OCEAN LIFE UP CLOSE

D0805181

Humpback Whales

by Christina Leaf

BLASTOFF!
READERS
3

BELLWETHER MEDIA · MINNEAPOLIS, MN

Note to Librarians, Teachers, and Parents:

Blastoff! Readers are carefully developed by literacy experts and combine standards-based content with developmentally appropriate text.

Level 1 provides the most support through repetition of high-frequency words, light text, predictable sentence patterns, and strong visual support.

Level 2 offers early readers a bit more challenge through varied simple sentences, increased text load, and less repetition of high-frequency words.

Level 3 advances early-fluent readers toward fluency through increased text and concept load, less reliance on visuals, longer sentences, and more literary language.

Level 4 builds reading stamina by providing more text per page, increased use of punctuation, greater variation in sentence patterns, and increasingly challenging vocabulary.

Level 5 encourages children to move from "learning to read" to "reading to learn" by providing even more text, varied writing styles, and less familiar topics.

Whichever book is right for your reader, Blastoff! Readers are the perfect books to build confidence and encourage a love of reading that will last a lifetime!

This edition first published in 2017 by Bellwether Media, Inc.

No part of this publication may be reproduced in whole or in part without written permission of the publisher. For information regarding permission, write to Bellwether Media, Inc., Attention: Permissions Department, 6012 Blue Circle Dr., Minnetonka, MN 55343.

Library of Congress Cataloging-in-Publication Data

Names: Leaf, Christina, author.
Title: Humpback Whales / by Christina Leaf.
Description: Minneapolis, MN : Bellwether Media, Inc., [2017] | Series:
   Blastoff! Readers. Ocean Life Up Close | Audience: Age 5-8. | Audience:
   Grade K to grade 3. | Includes bibliographical references and index.
Identifiers: LCCN 2015050510 | ISBN 9781626174177 (hardcover : alk. paper)
ISBN 9781618912657 (paperback : alk. paper)
Subjects: LCSH: Humpback whale–Juvenile literature.
Classification: LCC QL737.C424 L43 2017 | DDC 599.5/25–dc23
LC record available at http://lccn.loc.gov/2015050510

Printed in the United States of America, North Mankato, MN.

Table of Contents

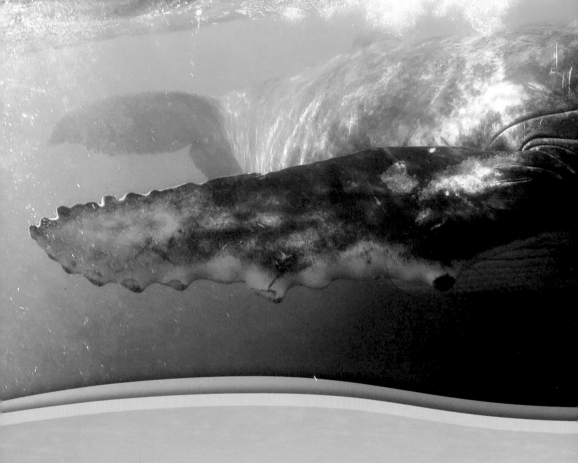

Humpback whales are huge **mammals** famous for their songs. Males sing together underwater.

Humans once hunted these animals until few remained. Today, humpbacks are protected. Their numbers are healthy and continue to grow.

breaching

blowholes

These whales mainly stay in shallow waters. Humpbacks must come to the surface to breathe. Their two **blowholes** take in air.

They also surface to **breach** or slap the water with their fins.

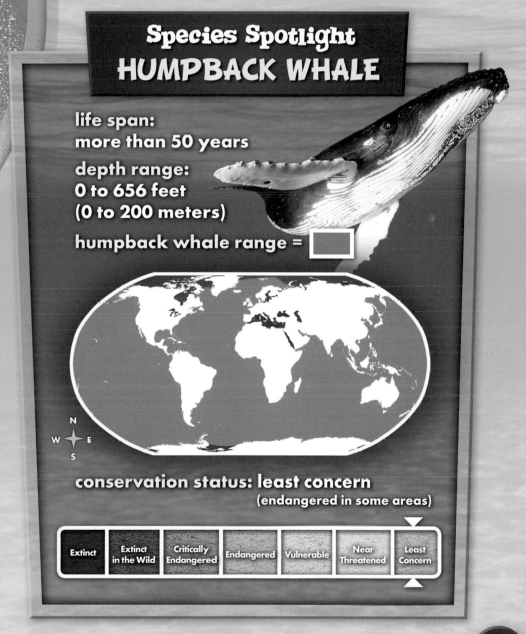

Species Spotlight
HUMPBACK WHALE

life span:
more than 50 years

depth range:
0 to 656 feet
(0 to 200 meters)

humpback whale range =

N
W ✦ E
S

conservation status: **least concern**
(endangered in some areas)

Extinct	Extinct in the Wild	Critically Endangered	Endangered	Vulnerable	Near Threatened	Least Concern

Humpback whales measure up to 62 feet (19 meters) long. They are longer than a school bus! Some weigh 40 tons (36 metric tons).

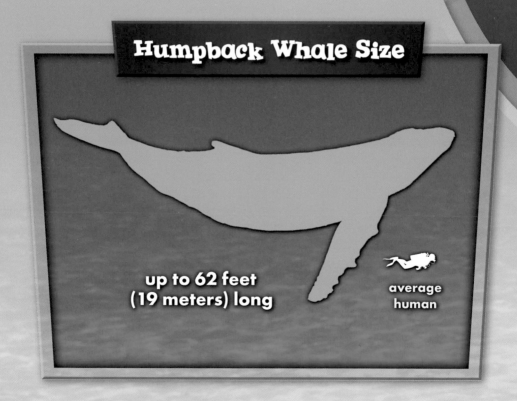

Humpback Whale Size

up to 62 feet
(19 meters) long

average
human

dorsal fin

The whale's name comes from the hump under its **dorsal fin**.

Their bodies are black or gray with some white on the underside. Humpback **flukes** each have their own special pattern.

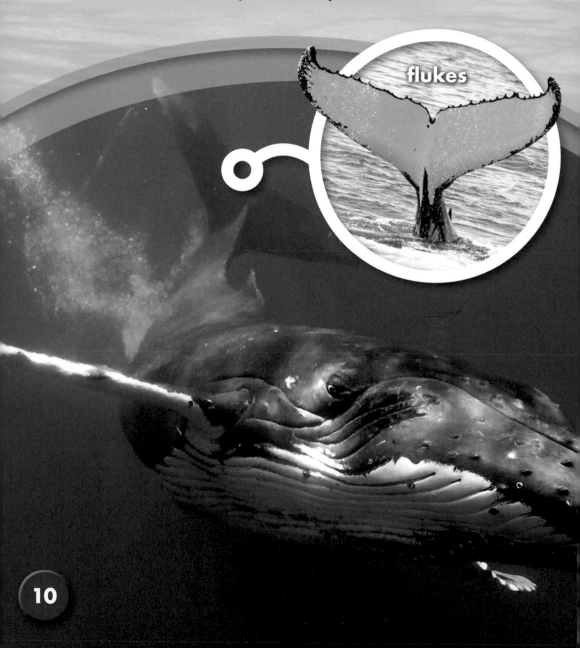

flukes

Identify a Humpback Whale

head bumps

long flippers

dorsal fin on hump

A long **flipper** is on each side of a humpback's body. Bumps dot humpbacks' heads.

Baleen and Bubble Nets

Humpback whales have comblike **baleen** instead of teeth. Baleen trap food inside their mouths.

Krill make up most of a humpback's diet. The **omnivores** also eat small fish and **plankton**.

Catch of the Day

Antarctic krill

Atlantic herring

capelins

baleen

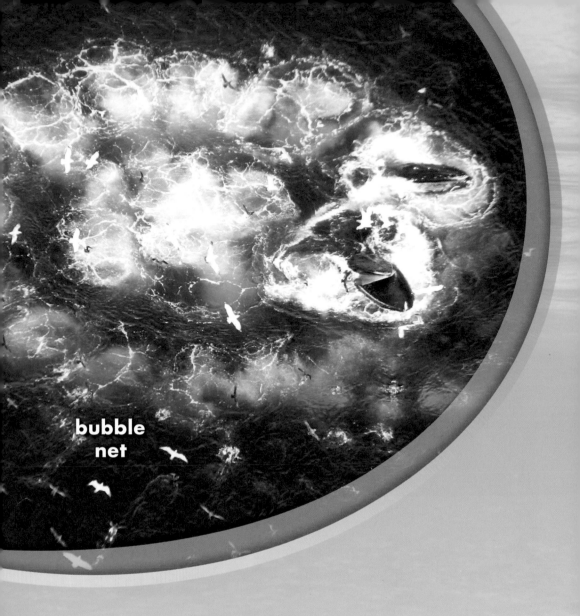

bubble
net

Some humpbacks hunt together.
They trap **prey** with a net of
bubbles. Whale noises help scare
the prey toward the surface.

Then the whales swim up for a big gulp of food.

Each year, most humpback whales travel thousands of miles. In summer, they **migrate** to chilly waters to find krill.

Humpback Whale Migration

summer feeding grounds =

winter breeding grounds =

N
W E
S

Some **pods** head south toward Antarctica. Others swim north to the **Arctic**.

In winter, the whales
return to warmer waters.
There, females give birth.
A female has one **calf**
every few years.

The calf stays close to mom for one year. The pair touches fins to show love.

Songs of the Deep

Male humpbacks may sing together for hours. All singers in an area know the same song.

Songs change with time. But why
humpbacks sing is a mystery.
Humans have much to learn
about these grand animals!

Glossary

Arctic—the cold region around the North Pole

baleen—plates of material that hang down from the top jaw of toothless whales

blowholes—the holes on top of a humpback whale's head that are used for breathing

breach—to leap out of the water

calf—a baby humpback whale

dorsal fin—the fin on top of a humpback whale's back

flipper—a flat, wide body part that is used for swimming

flukes—the two halves of a humpback whale's tail fin

mammals—warm-blooded animals that have backbones and feed their young milk

migrate—to travel from one place to another, often with the seasons

omnivores—animals that eat both plants and animals

plankton—ocean plants or animals that drift in water; most plankton are tiny.

pods—groups of humpback whales

prey—animals that are hunted by other animals for food

To Learn More

AT THE LIBRARY

Hirsch, Rebecca E. *Humpback Whales: Musical Migrating Mammals.* Minneapolis, Minn.: Lerner Publications Company, 2015.

O'Connell, Jennifer. *The Eye of the Whale: A Rescue Story.* Gardiner, Maine: Tilbury House Publishers, 2013.

Sayre, April Pulley. *Here Come the Humpbacks!* Watertown, Mass.: Charlesbridge, 2013.

ON THE WEB

Learning more about humpback whales is as easy as 1, 2, 3.

1. Go to www.factsurfer.com.

2. Enter "humpback whales" into the search box.

3. Click the "Surf" button and you will see a list of related web sites.

With factsurfer.com, finding more information is just a click away.

Index

The images in this book are reproduced through the courtesy of: Masa Ushioda/ Age Fotostock/ SuperStock, front cover, p. 7; Dave Fleetham/ Pacific Stock-Design Pics/ SuperStock, pp. 3, 9; Yann hubert, pp. 4-5, 11 (top left); Gudkov Andrey, pp. 6 (top), 11 (top center); TTstudio, p. 6 (bottom); mark higgins, p. 10 (top); Age Fotostock/ SuperStock, p. 10 (bottom); Ethan Daniels, p. 11 (top right, bottom); Dmytro Pylypenko, p. 13 (top left); Henrik Larsson, p. 13 (top center); Sergey Goruppa, p. 13 (top right); Vicki Beaver/ Alamy, p. 13 (bottom); Gulf of Maine Produc/ Age Fotostock, p. 14; Biosphoto/ SuperStock, p. 15; Deposit Photos/ Glow Images, p. 17; redbrickstock.com/ Alamy, p. 18; Marco Simoni/ Glow Images, p. 19; Flip Nicklin/ Minden Pictures/ SuperStock, pp. 20-21.